Handling Equine Patients

Other Works by Dr. Robert M. Miller

Books

Natural Horsemanship Explained – From Heart to Hands
The Revolution in Horsemanship (Co-authored with Rick Lamb)
Understanding the Ancient Secrets of the Horse's Mind
Imprint Training of the Newborn Foal
The Passion For Horses & Artistic Talent – An Unrecognized Connection
Mind Over Miller
Yes, We Treat Aardvarks

Equine Videos

Understanding Horses
Safer Horsemanship
Early Learning
Control of the Horse
Influencing the Horse's Mind
The Causes of Lameness

Cartoon Books

Am I Getting To Old For This?
The Second Oldest Profession
Ranchin' Ropin' an' Doctorin'
A Midstream Collection

Websites

www.robertmmiller.com
www.rmmcartoons.com
www.thepassionforhorses.com

Handling Equine Patients

A Handbook for Veterinary Students
and Veterinary Technicians

By Robert M. Miller D.V.M.

ISBN 978-0-9844620-2-5
Published by

Robert M. Miller Communications
14415 Donnington Lane
Truckee CA 96161
www.robertmmiller.com
email: info@robertmmiller.com

Cover Design by Silver Moon Graphics
www.silvermoongraphics.com

Thanks to my colleagues Doctors Glen "Andy" Anderson, Bill Moyer, and Betsy Connolly for their help with this book.

I especially want to express my appreciation to Dr. Marcia Thibeault for suggesting that I share the techniques described in this handbook with those who treat equine patients.

About The Cover Photo

Photographer Bonnie Edelman was introduced to Dr. Miller's method of imprint training 8 years ago on a trip to Uruguay. It was here that Bonnie says she found the most incredible, reliable, calm and almost human-like group of equines she had ever encountered. The imprinting technique was explained to Bonnie, which fascinated and intrigued her so much, that she found herself lying on her back one

morning, completely trusting the graceful animals grazing around her. It was then that Bonnie made what would be the first photograph of her Sermo per Equus series, called "Contineo, 2003". That very first photo graces the cover of this book.

Please visit www.bonnieedelman.com

Note: Dr. Miller wrote the forward to Bonnie's new book, "Sermo per Equus" published in 2010.

Table Of Contents

Introduction

The horse is the most dangerous of all veterinary patients. It is a prey species whose primary defense is flight. Hence, it is extremely perceptive, very swift, and physically strong, exceeding human abilities in these three qualities. That's why they so often injure people or injure themselves. Their timidity leads to sudden rapid and unexpected actions of either flight or fight. No matter how young and athletic we are, even an old and decrepit horse can move faster than we can and seriously injure us or a bystander.

In my lifetime I have known two colleagues killed by horses and some so severely injured that several had to give up large animal practice. Financial damage with subsequent lawsuits and insurance settlements are larger in equine practice than any other kind of practice. That's why insurance premiums are higher for equine practitioners than for other members of the profession. Also, the value of horses is usually higher than it is in other animals.

Horses, when frightened often damage themselves, hurt people, and destroy costly medical equipment such as digital radiography machines, endoscopes, ultrasonic devices, etc.

It is impossible to completely avoid such mishaps, but, the overwhelming majority of them can be avoided if the techniques described in this manual are rigidly followed. I think I am well qualified to say that the horse is the most dangerous of all veterinary patients. Few veterinarians have had the variety of patients as I did during my career.

I graduated from Colorado State University with a Doctor of Veterinary Medicine degree in 1956. For the next two years I worked for other veterinarians in mixed animal practice, mostly dogs, cats, cattle and horses.

Then, in 1958, I set up a practice in The Conejo Valley of California, a rural area that had never had a local resident practitioner. All veterinary services were imported from adjacent Los Angeles County, or elsewhere in Ventura County.

Although the human population of the valley was small, about 3000 people, the animal population was enormous. Thousands of beef cattle grazed the grasslands, and there were dozens of horse farms, some of them world class facilities.

The only industry in the valley other than ranching was the exotic animal industry which primarily served the motion picture and television business in nearby Los Angeles County.

There was a huge private zoo called "Jungleland" with an astounding collection of big cats, apes, and every other imaginable species.

Goebel and Son imported and exported zoo animals internationally. There was Bird Wonderland, which imported birds from all over the world. There was an elephant training center, a camel breeding farm and several wild animal farms used for making movies.

Behind my hospital the John Strong Family Circus was headquartered and other circuses stopped by on their circuits for veterinary services.

As it became known that we would treat all animals, a lot of clients brought in exotic pets from Los Angeles, such as ocelots, monkeys, and even full grown lions and tigers.

Soon Pacific Ocean Park, 55 miles away in Santa Monica, asked us to become their regular veterinarians for their dolphins, whales, chimpanzees, and sea lions.

Moorpark College, ten miles away, opened the world's only Collegiate Exotic Animal Management and Training program (EATM) which included a full-sized zoo and our practice served that school.

As a result I have waded into pools to treat dolphins, stepped into cages full of trained lions and other big cats to vaccinate them, done dentistry on fully conscious mature chimpanzees (the patient I fear most), sutured wounds on pythons and boa constrictors, tranquilized and anesthetized wild boars, and operated on a lumbar abscess on a full grown bull elephant while standing on an aluminum ladder.

Yet, I insist it is the horse that is the most difficult of all veterinary patients for the reasons cited earlier.

Difficult cattle are put into stanchions or chutes. Aggressive dogs are muzzled and cats put into a cat bag. But the veterinarian is expected to walk up to any horse, this large, strong, timid, swift creature and do things that are invariably frightening, or painful, or both.

Once I established my practice, it grew swiftly, and I added partners and associate veterinarians regularly. When I retired in 1988 there were 12 doctors in the group, the largest general practice in the USA at that time.

When the practice was ten years old and had four doctors, I gave up small animal surgery. This enabled me to spend more time in our rapidly growing horse practice.

A few years later I gave up hospital practice and did only ambulatory calls which were mostly, but not exclusively, equine.

Chapter 1

"We Need More Training"

During my veterinary education I received absolutely no training in animal behavior or how to handle our patients other than a course in "Restraint of Domestic Animals."

None of the later tranquilizing, immobilizing, and hypnotic drugs were yet available. Today many veterinary schools do have courses in animal behavior and, of course, students are taught the use of behavior modifying drugs in pharmacology, but the curriculum, saturated with today's technology, simply does not permit the proper teaching of handling horses. Few schools of either veterinary medicine or veterinary technology have faculty expertise in this vital field. We also realize that very few graduates will ever be required to handle equine patients. So, it is a neglected field and that is what motivated me to write this manual.

I must explain that I wasn't born with any special gift for handling horses. What I learned took me a lifetime, and in my mid eighties, I am still learning. What I do have is a great compulsion to share what I have learned, for the benefit of my colleagues, the horses, and those who own and love them.

The summer of 1947 I worked for a small ranch in Southern

1

Arizona. They had half a dozen colts to break and had hired a "bronc buster" to do the job.

I told him that I wished I knew how to do that and he kindly offered to show me. He picked a gentle 3 year old for me and showed me the routine.

It was very coercive and has been glorified and glamorized in art and prose and poetry. The horse was roped, tied down, blind folded, a leg tied up, saddled and then you got on it and tried to stay on until it stopped bucking.

Although this was traditional and much admired, what I saw was the terror in that colt's eyes and I knew there had to be a better way. When I got back at the end of the summer to Tucson to go to school, I talked to several horse trainers. They all agreed that this method was appropriate and traditional.

So, I went to the town library and the University of Arizona library and found some old books that gave me clues as to a more humane and civilized method. I thought about it for the next three years.

Meanwhile, I decided to study veterinary medicine, hopefully in Colorado, so I started looking for summer jobs in that state.

I started colts the last four summers before I graduated veterinary school, and what I did was almost exactly what is being done today by horsemen active in what I call "The Revolution in Horsemanship."

In 2005, with co-author Rick Lamb, I wrote a book with that title (Lyons Press).

In 1987, I retired from veterinary practice to join the revolution which teaches how to train horses without the use of force, using instead kindness, consideration, psychology, gentleness, and intelligence. This quarter century old movement is changing the millennial old art of horsemanship forever. The knowledge is now available for everybody, rather than for a few rare, privileged individuals.

The colts I started were usually 4 or 5 years of age. Some were wild and had never been handled or had human contact. Others had been caught up as yearlings, branded and castrated if male. None were halter broke.

The way I handled these horses is pertinent to the theme of this book. My goal was to minimize fear and never to justify it. At the same time I wanted complete respect. That should be the goal in our relationship with horses - 100% respect and zero fear, a probably unattainable goal, but one which can be achieved far more so than is done using traditional methods.

Once a colt was isolated from the herd (a terrifying experience) it would stampede around the pen, sometimes crashing the fence or trying to jump it. Every ranch had a round "breaking" pen, with a well worn snubbing post in the center. I never used the post.

My first goal was to alleviate fear, so I just sat outside the pen with my back to the colt (a non-predatory position) for 10 or 15 minutes. At the end of that time the colt would be shaking with fear, but standing still.

The next day I repeated this experience, this time sitting inside the pen. At the end of this session the colt would be apprehensive, but calm, and observing me from a distance.

The third lesson, the now more relaxed colt would be roped. This precipitated another stampeding flight reaction, but it soon terminated and the colt would finally stand still. I then applied pressure to the lariat at an angle until the colt took a step toward me. This was repeated in both directions until it learned that the greatest comfort was to face me. I didn't know until 30 years later that a generation before me, an Australian named Kell Jeffery had developed an identical technique for starting colts.

The next lesson consisted of slowly and non-aggressively stepping toward the horse. As soon as I saw tension and fear, I would step back a step or two. This immediately relieves the fear and aborts flight. Predators do not retreat.

Eventually, I was able to get right up to the horse and allow it to smell my hand.

Next came the most dangerous part of the entire procedure, because I would attempt to lightly touch the face. This often caused the horse to strike at me with its forelegs. However, using caution, patience and persistence I was soon stroking the head and neck.

At this point I felt that my mission was largely accomplished. The most difficult part was over. I had gained the frightened animal's confidence and trust.

I went on to progressively rub the horse's entire body, taking as long as a full hour to do so. I also picked up, gently and briefly, each leg. Then, I rubbed the horse with a rope, a sack, and finally a McClellan cavalry saddle I could hold in one hand. A surcingle with a cinch attached was put around the girth area and repetitiously tightened for at least 100 pulls, gradually increasing the force.

Then, a stock saddle was put on the horse and he was taught to turn in each direction, to move forward on command, and to back up.

This was done from the ground in a halter or a hackamore. I did not use a bit until the colt had been ridden many times.

Finally, I carefully mounted and dismounted several times, and soon I was riding the horse. This was usually by the seventh to the ninth day. Each day's lesson was longer, starting with 10 or 15 minutes, and working up to a full hour.

Never once did any of those colts buck when it was mounted. Some did when first saddled, and a few did a couple of weeks later when frightened, but none did for the first rides.

I rode them in the round pen 3 or 4 times. Then, they were ridden in a large corral perhaps 3 or 4 times. After that I tried to get them right out moving cattle, always trying to put them in back of the herd so cattle were moving away from the horse. This gave them confidence. Why? Because predators do not retreat. While I rode, I'd play with a rope, tossing it at the cattle's back and hind legs.

The result was a broke cowhorse with no agitation, bucking or frantic battles. I came up with this method on my own, inspired by the desire not to frighten the horse.

Then, finally, I graduated veterinary school. I was 30 years of age and I never started another colt except for a couple of dozen for my wife and I that we had either purchased or raised ourselves. These included both horses and mules.

My practice included horses from the beginning. Rarely was this an unbroke horse, except for young foals. Most were at least halter broke, and a majority were mature riding horses.

Completely ignoring the effective colt starting method I had thought out so carefully, I went right to work handling equine patients the way I was taught in school. Back then the "bread and butter" of horse practice was "tube worming." Twice a year the horse was twitched, a 10-foot long nasogastric tube inserted into a nostril and passed down the stomach, and phenothiazine or carbon disulfide, the only vermifuges then available, was pumped into the horse.

Each time a patient was seen a greater level of fear and resistance was usually exhibited.

Of course, the tranquilizing drugs had not yet been discovered.

In 1959, my third year of practice, I made two huge discoveries which would change my Life

One was that I learned newborn foals could be trained and would permanently retain what they were taught. This epiphany will be discussed later.

The other discovery came more gradually. I had noticed that when I had to do a routine physical examination on a well broke, gentle, mature horse, that when I listened to its heart with a stethoscope that it was usually pounding.

I slowly began to realize that this was an adrenalin reaction. Even though those horses had learned to stand quietly while I did a routine insurance exam, or an interstate travel exam, or a pre-purchase exam, THEY WERE FRIGHTENED!

Eventually, realizing this, I decided to use the same approach with my patients that I had with those wild colts before I graduated. I was going to minimize fear.

What I am going to describe in the following chapter made my life so much easier, so less filled with conflict, so much safer for me, the patient, and any bystanders.

Chapter 2

"Initial Approach"

We are always in a hurry. Veterinarians usually start the day with a full schedule and in horse practice, the chances are that some sort of emergency or a demanding client will disrupt that schedule.

So, we move rapidly when we arrive at a farm or stable. Especially if we are male, and are young, we usually walk toward the horse with a determined rolling gait, and usually we are carrying equipment. This is intimidating to many horses.

In my third year of practice, I learned not to do this. I learned that slower is faster.

I would get out of my vehicle casually. When it was time to approach the horse, I walked quietly. I did not stare at him. This is predatory. Instead, I looked to the side and angled my body somewhat aside. A direct approach is predatory. I carried nothing and kept my hands relaxed. A closed fist is predatory, and don't think horses don't notice your hands.

As I approached the horse I slumped and made myself smaller. I focused on his foreleg and when next to it I quietly rubbed the shoulder and withers. I rubbed until I saw, through my peripheral vision, the head lowered its position. I rubbed the withers, then the neck, and finally the face.

If the horse's head came up, a flight reaction, I'd retreat with my rubbing to where he was more relaxed. Predators don't retreat.

All of this would take from half a minute to a couple of minutes. I'd wait for the sigh, what I called "the let down," before I finally made eye contact with the horse.

If all this failed to reassure the horse, or if I thought this procedure was going to take ten minutes or longer, I knew I would have to use another method, perhaps chemical or physical restraint.

But, the majority of equine patients can be reassured and made more cooperative by simply using a friendlier and less intimidating approach.

Most people choose horse practice because they love horses. Take the time to let the horse know this.

Horses are so perceptive that they quickly size us up and a little affection and reassurance go a long way.

Also, before beginning the examination or treatment, it's a good idea to take the lead rope and walk the horse around in a circle, back up a couple of steps, go forward, then back up again.

Why do we do this? Because, horses establish their dominance by controlling movement of their peers. Showing the horse that you control its movement helps to establish you as a leader, rather than as a predator. Control the horse's feet and you control his mind. All of this should not take more than a minute or two, but it often makes all that follows easier.

However, when doing this do not allow the horse to control the speed or direction in which you are going. That would negate our goal of establishing our role as a leader. By changing directions and insisting that the horse be properly positioned and not leading us around, we help to establish our dominance in the horse's mind.

Preparing to temp a strange horse, I stand at the shoulder with close contact. Look at my left foot, extended so I can lean to the right with my foot contacting the horse's Fetlock. I test the perineum.

If all seems well I slide towards the hindquarters, my hip pressed against the horse's stifle, and rotate the thermometer which encourages the sphincter to relax

Same procedure on another patient. Close contact, my left
leg blocking his, and ready to take temperature.

Chapter 3

"Chemical Restraint"

I tranquilized the fIrst horse to receive such a drug in California. I injected Promazine and seeing the profound sedation that resulted, in a very diffIcult 17 hand tall Thoroughbred hunter, made me realize that we were beginning a new era in equine medicine.

During the following decades, I did clinical trials for the pharmaceutical industry using several such drugs, such as xylazine and detomidine. These and other behavior modifying drugs have been an indescribable boon to the equine practitioner. However, they are used excessively and often unnecessarily. All drugs have potential side effects. Having given countless thousands of doses of such medications, I have seen the adverse side effects which has made me cautious and conservative about using them. As described in the previous chapter, sometimes a few minutes spent getting acquainted with the horse and establishing a relationship removes the necessity for using any of these drugs.

However, when we need them they can be a great help to the horse practitioner.

One thing I learned is that these drugs do not interfere with the learning ability of the horse. Indeed, I believe they can actually enhance learning by diminishing the fear and emotion that often elicit misbehavior in our equine patients.

So, for example, I may give a horse a dose of acepromazine in order to facilitate dentistry.

Then, the next time dentistry is needed I'll give half the original dose. I'll halve it again the third time and thereafter the horse will typically accept the procedure, the drug having overcome the fear response.

Be careful when working around horses sedated with xylazine. They sometimes suddenly startle and may kick or even strike without warning.

Always be careful where you stand in relationship to the horse.

One word of advice. After a horse is sedated, continue to handle it in a manner that will not precipitate a flight or fight response. In other words, work on the tranquilized horse as if it were not tranquilized. This may avert an undesirable response.

Chapter 4

" Physical Restraint"

The primary theme of this manual is that if we approach horses in a calm, quiet, placid, reassuring manner, and take the time to placate them, we can frequently abort the fearful flight or flight instincts which make many horses difficult patients.

However, just as we admitted in the previous chapter, the use of behavior controlling chemicals are often justified, we must also admit that control through the use of physical restraint is also often necessary.

Basically there are three functions in physical restraint:

I.   Mechanical immobilization
II. Inhibition through pain
III. Creating submission by controlling movement

Lets consider each of these separately even though there is some overlap in the effects of these techniques.

I. Mechanical Immobilization

This can include complete immobilization of the horse's body. Examples include:
  A. Confining the horse within a chute or stocks. Farms and stables should always be encouraged to construct such a facility and, importantly train the horse to enter it quietly and willingly. This should be done <u>before</u> any veterinary treatment is required, just as horses should be trained to load into a horse trailer routinely, and <u>not</u> until transportation to a show or hospital or a stud farm is imminent.
  B. Casting the horse (tying it down on the ground)
  C. Mechanical immobilization can consist of hobbling one or more legs, or confining the patient for treatment behind a gate or in a horse trailer.

II. Inhibition through pain

Inflicting sudden pain upon a horse as with a lip twitch, an ear hold, grasping a fold of skin, or applying pressure to the underside of the upper lip with a cord, rope, or chain will usually cause temporary immobilization. The twitch is the most familiar device used to control horses for veterinary procedures.

The twitch is an entirely justifiable and useful tool. However, it can be misused and overused. When I started practice, I used the twitch all day long because I had been trained to do so in school.

Twenty years later I probably twitched a horse once a week, and I know colleagues who have completely given up the use of the twitch.

I was taught in school that the twitch's effect is due to inhibition through pain. Similar techniques are used in the martial arts for humans.

Recently, studies have shown that endorphins are produced by the brain when a twitch is applied, and it is suggested that the immobilizing effect derived is due to the calming effects of the endorphins.

This is nonsense. Of <u>course</u>, endorphins are elaborated when pain is inflicted, but they take <u>time</u> to take effect. The twitch usually produces immediate (but temporary) immobilization. It is <u>after</u> the endorphins cause analgesia that the twitch wears off, typically after several minutes.

So, we are deluding ourselves if we believe that a twitched horse stands still because he feels good. He stands still because movement and reaction are aborted by <u>PAIN</u>. It works and it is sometimes necessary, but pain is the reason this method should be minimally used, especially if more humane methods are available.

Moreover, the lip twitch is not the only method of obtaining immobilization through pain. A traditional cowboy trick is to bite the ear of a refractory horse. It works, but veterinary personnel don't want to use such a crass method. A twitch can be applied to the ear, but I disapprove of doing this. Instead, the ear can be grasped with the fingertips, squeezed hard, and <u>not twisted</u>, but pulled straight down. Many clients disapprove of this and I rarely used it, especially in front of a client but it <u>works</u>.

In my video, <u>Control of the Horse - The Art of Restraint</u> (Video Horse World, 1994), which is largely concerned with physical restraint, I teach how to apply a twitch, or an ear hold, or twisting the skin over the shoulder so as <u>not to make the horse refractory to such methods in the future</u>.

It is simply a question of sandwiching the restraint method, which <u>is</u> painful, in between two very pleasant experiences. What I do is take lots of time, gently massage the part to be twitched for a long time until the horse shows complete relaxation and enjoyment. Then, I gradually increase the pressure to immobilize the horse. Finally, when finished, I reverse the procedure, ending up with a gentle and pleasurable massage.

Using this technique, I can repeatedly "ear" or twitch my mules and mules are notoriously less forgiving and more suspicious than horses.

If a patient must be twitched do not demand complete immobility. Horses are claustrophobic creatures and if slight movements are permitted are less likely to suddenly "blow up" then if they are totally immobilized.

III. Creating submission by controlling movement

We stated earlier that the horse establishes its dominance hierarchy by controlling the movement of its peers. Movement (Flight) is the horse's primary defense against predators. It has no horns or tusks. So, to deprive it of flight produces submissiveness just as control of the head (the horns) makes cattle submissive. You'll see a ring in a bull's nose, but not in a horse's nose. We use head gates to control cattle, but to do that to a horse would probably cause a broken neck.

Control the feet and you control the horse's brain. Movement can be controlled in two ways: by causing it or by inhibiting it. That's why earlier, I advised walking the horse around in a circle and turning it and backing it before commencing treatment. It tells the horse you are in charge and makes resistance less likely.

Conversely, submissiveness is also obtained by preventing movement. That's why we should never treat an unhaltered horse. If the horse is properly halter broke (not all are), the moment the halter is put on the horse it realizes that flight is inhibited and it elevates our status as a leader. It creates respect.

More dramatically, hobbling horses (assuming they are trained to the hobbles) will produce submissiveness if they are left on long enough. That's why I think every horse should, early in its training, learn to stand quietly with conventional fore-leg hobbles, with one hind leg tied up with a "Scotch Hobble" and also with the Rarey Leg Strap.

Once a horse is well trained to hobbles, it need not be hobbled again until necessary. Even years later it will remember, accept the hobbles, and become submissive. That's why I think every young horse should be "hobble broke." It is a positive learning experience and may someday be needed.

A side benefit to "hobble breaking" is that, if the subject is ever accidently tangled in rope or wire, it is less likely to make frantic efforts to escape which usually increases trauma. A properly hobble horse broke is more likely to calmly wait for a human to untangle it.

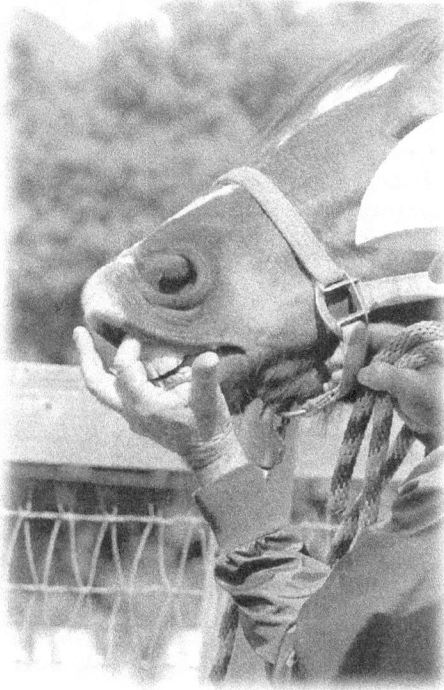

1. Preparing a horse for twitching, I first gain relaxation by massaging under the lip.

2. Then I gently massage the lip, very gradually increasing pressure.

3. Now Twitched by hand I start
To tighten the twitch.

4. Completely twitched.

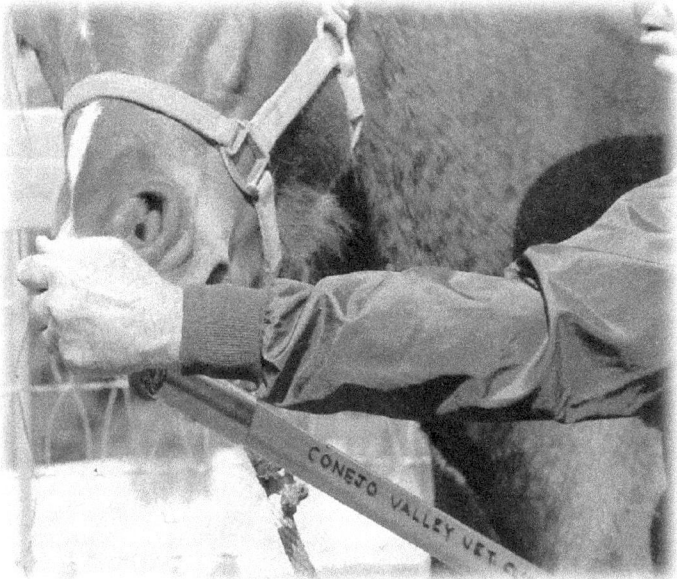

5. Loosening Twitch I reverse the procedure

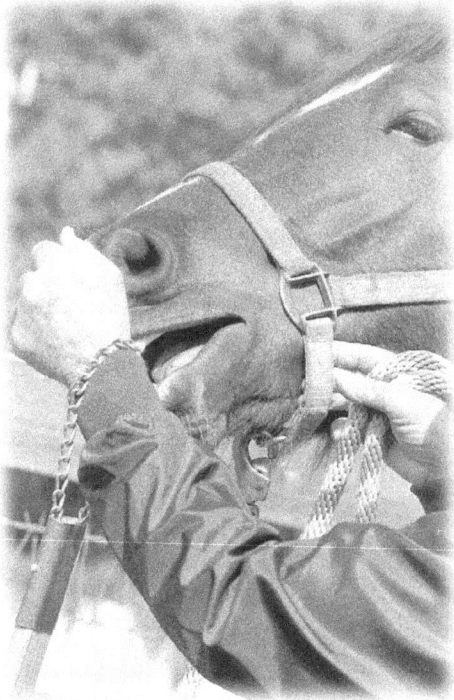

6. Twitch is now released and I finish with
a comforting gentle massage.

7. Using a clamp Twitch (a few minutes later) I repeat the same procedure

8. Now Twitched by hand.

9. Now applying clamp Twitch

10. Twitched and to remove it I will
reverse the entire process.

11. "Earing" a horse is done exactly the same
way. Begin with massage

12. Pull straight down, do not twist.

13. Twitching a horse with a shoulder skin hold
is done the same way.

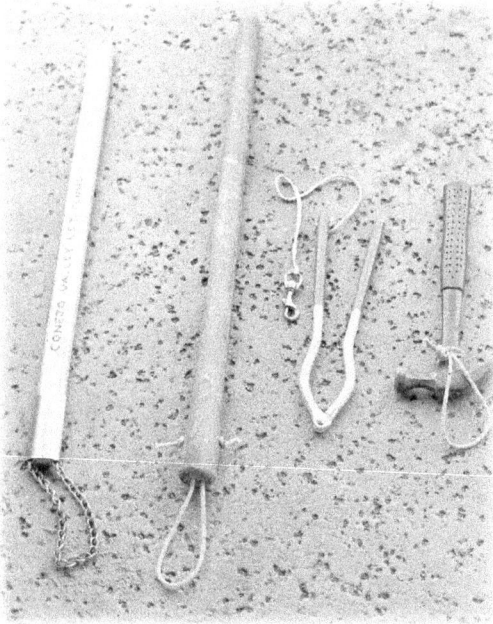

14. Various
Twitches including
one improvised
from a hammer
and loop of cord.

15. A mule hobbled with the one leg Rarey Strap.

Chapter 5

"Some Methods of
Modifying Behavior"

Pressure under the upper lip caused by a chain, or cord, or a rope can have several effects upon horses:

First of all, slow gentle pressure has a sedating effect. This has been explained as the result of an acupuncture point under the upper lip. Secondly, it has been claimed to cause a calming endorphin release. Placing a fairly heavy chain under the lip and then stepping back will, in most horses, cause the head to nod, the eyes to begin to look sleepy, and to assume a rather sedated expression. I found that I can accomplish the same thing by simply massaging under the lip. This is especially useful prior to examining or treating the mouth. Horses seem to enjoy pressure in this area.

The lip chain can be used in three ways:

A - to calm and distract the horse as just described

B - to immobilize the horse by applying strong pressure to the chain.

This creates inhibition through pain, just as a twitch does. Early in my career, I largely gave up the twitch for the lip chain for this reason: A twitch causes either slight pain or severe pain depending upon how it is used, but it is never free of pain.

C- A lip chain can cause pleasure if very little pressure is caused, or slight pain if more pressure is used, or very severe pain if a lot of pressure is used. It therefore is a useful device for modifying behavior, whereas a twitch is always uncomfortable. It never feels good.

The lip chain can effectively be used to counter condition a horse.

Counter-conditioning is a technique used to extinguish a habitual undesirable behavior by creating a new and desirable response. For example, in one of my earliest videos, Influencing the Horse's Mind (palomine Productions, 1984} I am presented with a head shy horse. Any attempt to examine his teeth or mouth, or work on his head causes violent head tossing. What I did was gently apply a lead chain under his lip and quietly wait for him to find comfort in it. Then, I try to open his mouth. This caused a violent head toss, but since I am holding the chain lead with my other hand, this results in a sudden severe pain. I didn't do it. He did it to himself. I pet him and express sympathy.

This scenario is repeated three times. He doesn't blame me. He did it. Horses learn quickly. Three times does it. He has now been counter-conditioned and is afraid to toss his head, so he allows me to open his mouth. He has chosen the lesser of two evils. Now, he learns that my examining his mouth is a painless procedure. He softens and accepts me as a friend rather than as a predator.

In the video, again using the chain to counter-condition his head shyness, we go on to pass a nasogastric tube and to worm the horse without the use of tranquilizers or a twitch.

Importantly, he will remember this experience indefinitely, and providing that I repeat it in exactly the same manner, I will henceforth be able to work on his mouth or pass a tube to deworm him.

The same horse is also "goosey" and will not allow his temperature to be taken rectally.

Again, counter-conditioning him with the lip chain, it only takes a few times to teach him to stand still when I touch the base of his tail.

Then, using a habituation technique, I repeatedly stroke and rub his tail and perineal area until all fear and reaction is gone. I am careful to never act aggressive or let him know that I am responsible for his lip pain when he acts badly. He has to think that his own behavior is causing his discomfort and that I am there solely as a source of comfort and sympathy.

If done correctly, counter-conditioning can change a horse's behavior with remarkable speed and permanence.

It is so much better than fighting them, and so much safer.

Another use of the lip chain is for distraction. Horses can only think of one thing at a time, so gently vibrating the chain, many horses will ignore things like injections. We'll mention this technique again later.

Whenever a lip chain is used do not "hang onto it" with steady unyielding pressure. To do so may cause the horse to explosively flip over backwards.

APPLYING THE LIP CHAIN

Massaging the gum under the upper lip to relax
the horse and prepare it for the chain

After chain is applied I wait for the horse to relax
further, avoiding uncomfortable pressure

Chapter 6

"Defensive Horsemanship"

Most people are injured by gentle horses. We tend to be very wary when around known dangerous horses. So, it is the usually docile horse that injures us, most often due to a sudden defensive move precipitated by fear.

Also, more people are injured on the ground than when riding. This is of particular significance to veterinary personnel.

There are two places where one is safer around horses. One is <u>very far away</u>. The other is <u>very close</u>. Most injuries come from the in-between distances. If we are arm's distance from a horse, we are obviously also within leg's length.

Anybody that works with horses should develop habits of where to stand. Carelessness in this regard accounts for most injuries. As a general rule, whenever possible, the assistant to the person treating the horse should be on the same side.

In 1987, the recent graduate who replaced me when I retired from our practice got kicked so severely it ended her practice career. Then, one of my neighbors, an experienced rider, was <u>killed</u> by his gentle horse. I decided to make another video. "<u>Safer Horsemanship</u>", (Video Velocity, 1999), will save lives. It already has, I've been told. There are a few hints in it I'd like to emphasize here:

1. Work around <u>every</u> horse as if the unexpected will occur. If it does and you are properly positioned, you have a much better chance of escaping injury.

2. The shoulder of the horse is the safest place from which to work. The most probable injury is to get your toes stepped on. This is rarely fatal. But, keep in mind, if working on mules, that any mule can kick with its hind leg <u>beyond</u> its shoulder. Most horses can't or won't. Don't worry about soiling your clothes. Laundering is simpler than orthopedic surgery. If your body is contacting the horse (and, I like to maintain three points of contact, such as an arm, a hip, and perhaps my leg), you can feel the horse and he can feel you. If you are working on one side of a horse, the animal can only see you with the peripheral vision of one eye. Feeling you is reassuring. The horse wonders what you are doing and is often afraid. That contact will often prevent a sudden move from fear.

If I need to work on the hind quarters of a horse, I start at the shoulder and slide my body along the horses body until I reach the area I need. If I feel the horse clutch up from fear, I slide <u>back</u> toward the withers where I <u>started</u>. Remember, predators don't retreat, so this reassures the horse.

I use my arms and elbows to protect my face and head and this is nicely shown in that video.

During a career that included tens of thousand of horses, only once was I hospitalized and that was when a 90-day-old foal ran into me and damaged one of my knees. Yes, I had a lot of close calls, and, yes, I had some injuries not requiring hospitalization, and, yes, some of it was luck, but mainly I avoided injury by using the techniques described in this book.

THREE POINTS OF CONTACT

1. Medicating the eye when an assistant is not available, I push with left arm, open the eyelids with the left hand, pull with the right arm placed through a very loose halter, and squeeze the ointment tube between thumb and forefinger of the right hand. My left hip is pressed against the horse

2. Examining the inguinal area, I hold up a foreleg to discourage kicking and press both shoulders and my chest against the horse.

3. Working from the safety position at the shoulder (note my left foot and left arm) I test the horses reaction to having the left hind leg touched.
→

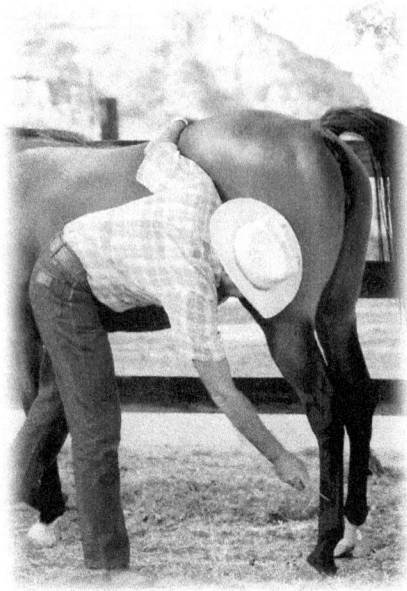

4. I ask for the foot to be lifted. Note the 3 points of contact. (left foot, left hip, and left arm)
←

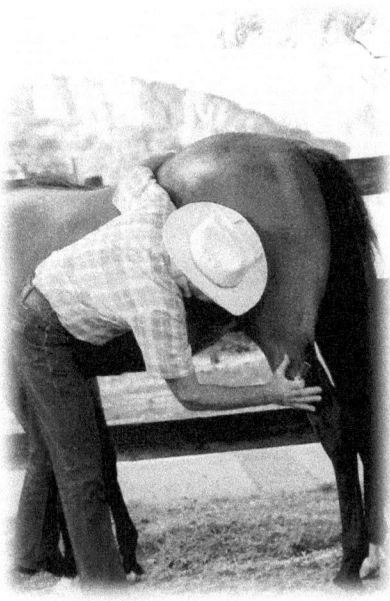

5. Now, I pick up the foot.
→

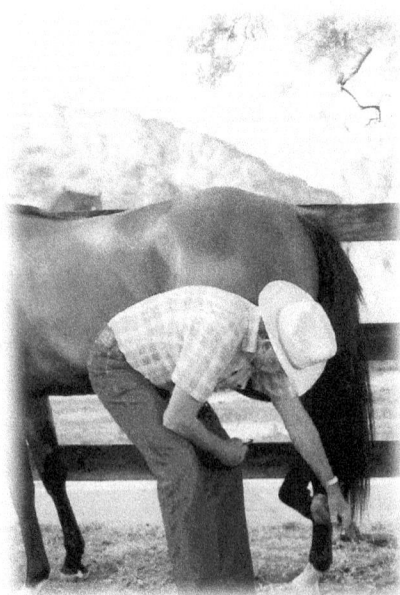

PREPARING A MARE FOR PALPATION

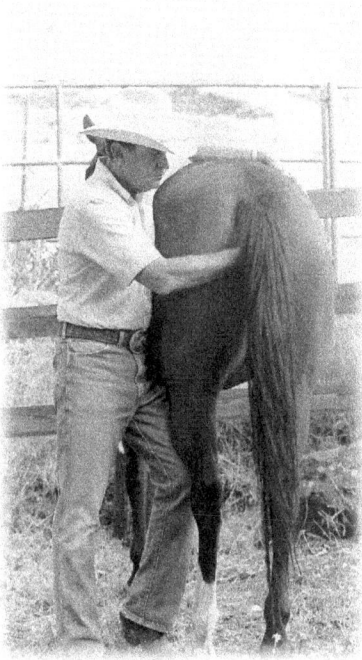

6. I am desensitizing the perineal region by rubbing until she in unconcerned and raises her tail. Note the points of contact. My left arm, entire left side and my left thigh contact her. My left hip is pressed against her stifle, inhibiting her ability to kick. My left knee blocks her hock for the same reason. Note that my left toe is in contact with her left hind foot.

7. Working on a forefoot I have 3 points of contact: My right arm, my right thigh, and my left hand. Closer is safer.

Chapter 7

"Patience and Persistence"

If we just slow down when working with horses, it can save us so much time.

I am naturally impatient and a very kinetic person, so it was not easy for me to learn this.

Horses taught me patience and persistence.

So many veterinary procedures can be done on horses and they can actually learn to enjoy them. Horses are a mutual grooming species, so they can enjoy any painless rhythmic tactile stimulus, once their fear is quelled. Let me give some examples: horses that have been used with a bridle bit are used to having metal in their mouth. So, I have been able to teach many horses to accept having their teeth floated with a dental rasp by simply gently inserting the rasp into the comer of the mouth. It helps to put some syrup or molasses on the blade. I let them mouth it for a while, and then, quietly move the rasp along the molars with the smooth back of the blade contacting the teeth. Stroke gently. As soon as the horse's posture and attitude tell me that his apprehension is gone and has been replaced with curiosity, I slowly reverse the blade and slowly begin to rasp the teeth. Soon the horse appears mesmerized by the slow rhythmic movements and then, I gradually increase the force. I have taught the horse to enjoy simple dentistry.

In the video mentioned earlier ("Influencing the Horse's Mind"), you can see how quickly the head shy, goosey gelding learns to enjoy a tube up his nose and a thermometer up his rear end.

As long as there is no pain, horses can be taught to tolerate <u>ANY</u> stimulus, no matter how severe. That's why horses were so vital in human warfare. Teeth floating, nasogastric intubation, rectal palpation, cleaning the sheath and many, many other routine procedures are <u>not</u> painful. So, in theory, if the horse can be convinced not to fear the procedure, most will do so. Those who require an inordinately long period of time can, of course be controlled by chemical or physical restraint methods mentioned earlier. In addition, there are many other tricks to speed the horse's acceptance of frightening procedures. For example, before administrating paste vermifuges, it is really simple to load a syringe with apple sauce and teach a horse to <u>enjoy</u> it. Clients can be taught to do this at home for several days prior to paste worming.

Occasionally, horses have to be given medications in bolus form. If the bolus is wrapped in thin tissue paper and deposited far back on the tongue, it encourages the swallowing reflex. For several years boluses were the state-of-the-art wormer and we administered thousands of doses this way. What we did was to hold the paper-wrapped blolus between the second and third fingers and introduce our hand into the mouth through the interdental space. (In male horses the canine tooth sometimes causes a problem here). The hand is then pushed over the tongue and the bolus deposited as far back as possible in the throat. The tissue paper seems to stimulate the swallowing reflex. We found this method very superior to the use of a balling gun.

Preparing a colt for examination of the mouth

I begin by massaging the gums than I gently grasp the tongue ↑ and visually examine the mouth. By this time I have the colt's confidence so I can insert my hand ↓ to palpate the cheek teeth.

Chapter 8

"Creating Cooperative Patients"

We are not horse trainers, nor should our clientele expect us to be. However, it <u>is</u> incumbent upon us not to cause behavior problems that can last the horse's lifetime. So, we have to <u>choose</u> the approach that will be safest for us, safest for the horse, and not create future problems.

It is certainly appropriate for us to advise the client as to what can be done to improve a specific horse's behavior.

As described in the last chapter, for example, the client can teach a horse to be prepared for paste worming by using apple sauce, or sweet syrup. Clients can teach horses to allow rubbing and handling of any and all body parts. It just takes some time. There really is no excuse for head shy, ear shy, or "goosey" horses. It is so easy to desensitize them if we know how.

The single greatest thing I did in my practice to create a predominantly cooperative patient load was to imprint train their newborn foals. After I conceived of this method in 1959, I took every opportunity to demonstrate it to my clients, usually during a routine postpartum examination. I never charged for this, although, it typically took an hour or more because a) I knew that the foal would be a good patient forever more, and, b) it would encourage many clients to do this with every future foal, after they saw how the foal I worked on behaved afterwards.

This manual is not the place to describe what I call imprint training, which is training during the foal's imprinting period which is as soon as they are born.

Puppies are an ALTRICIAL species. They are born helpless and don't imprint (bond with whatever they see moving near them) until six weeks of age.

Human babies are also an ALTRICIAL species.

But, horses are a PRECOCIAL species. They are born neurologically mature with senses functional, and their peak learning time in life is in the hours and days after they enter this world.

Other precocial species include cattle, sheep, goats, geese, ducks, turkeys, quail, antelope, buffalo, and so on. These species will bond with whatever is seen moving around them right after birth.

For information about imprint training, the most effective and fastest way to create good equine patients, I have done several books and videos on the subject since I stumbled upon it over half a century ago:

Video: Imprint Training of the Newborn Foal, Palomine Productions, 1986

Video: Early Learning, Video Velocity, 1995

Book: Imprint Training of the Newborn Foal, Western Horseman, 1991

Book: Understanding the Ancient Secrets of the Horse's Mind, Russel Meerdink Co., 2000

If done correctly, imprint training is 100% effective. I have not had a failure in over fifty years, and many of those horses ended up as racing or show champions.

It sure made my life easier.

I also encouraged all breeding farms with three or more mares to install a palpating chute and to take the time to teach the mares to enter it and stand quietly. I would charge more for my services if a farm refused to provide a chute.

When working with the newborn foals, many people allow the mare to observe the process unhaltered. I do not recommend this. Always have a halter on the mare and have her handled by a competent person. This is in case of unexpected aggression by the mare. True, I have never experienced this when imprint training a foal, but it is better to be safe than sorry. It will also help to prevent the mare accidentally stepping on the foals legs. And, as always, controlling movement in horses generates respect.

1. Working with a 15 minute old foal in a ranch pasture

2. Second training session with a 24 hour old foal. It is completely relaxed and compliant and will remain so if not mishandled.

3. I am habituating the mouth, including gums, teeth, and tongue to human handling. This just born foal will grow up to be a good patient.

4. Desensitizing the ear, including the pinna and the ear canal to manipulation. It takes 50 to 100 rapid, gentle stimuli, and each ear must be done because the results are very specific.

5. Desensitizing a 24 hour old foal to electric clippers.

6. At one week of age this foal leads from her dam
lightly and willingly

Chapter 9

"Hospital Practice"

My experience in equine practice was entirely ambulatory. We never had a large animal hospital, but referred patients as needed to several facilities accessible from our town. We did see horses brought to our small animal hospital in trailers. This often included radiography, ultrasonic physical therapy, acupuncture, minor surgeries and so on, but cases like these rarely exceeded once a day. Nearly all of our equine patients were seen on an ambulatory basis and during most of the time I practiced we had two or three well equipped mobile units for this purpose and also a unit equipped solely for radiography. We would write a prescription for our X-rays and one of our technicians would go out and take the pictures. This, of course, was before the advent of digital radiography.

Except during after-hours emergencies, a veterinary technician nearly always rode with our doctors. It greatly increased our efficiency.

So, although my experience with hospitalized horses was mostly limited to the days I was a veterinary student, I am quite familiar with the problems of handling hospitalized horses and especially with handling post-operative patients. Too often major surgery is performed upon a horse successfully, only to have the horse destroy itself postoperatively.

Hospital personnel, from doctors to assistants to the person who cleans the stall must understand these things:

1. The horse is in a strange and frightening environment. We must have empathy.

2. The horse probably feels ill, or is in pain. The pain is often post operative and was not present beforehand, or, at least not as severe.

3. The hospitalized horse is usually confined to a stall. This may not be what he was used to at home. If the horse is used to more space, the confinement can be extremely stressful.

4. Chances are that the horse is never alone at home. Isolation is unnatural for an animal meant to live in herds, and if suddenly imposed upon him, the anxiety and stress can be huge.

5. Added to all of the above, strangers keep entering the stall, often dressed in unfamiliar hospital apparel and carrying unfamiliar equipment and objects. Then, usually, treatments are administered which are often uncomfortable and frequently painful.

When all of the above is considered it can be easily understood why some horses damage themselves when hospitalized. Some undo surgical repairs. Others injure people trying to help them.

What can be done to minimize post operative trauma, rehab problems, and stress during hospitalization?

1. Every single hospital staff member should understand and utilize the principles of handling horses discussed in the preceding chapters.

2. Each horse is different and "one stall for all" may not suffice. Some patients may require more room, or visual access to other horses. Some may require a particularly safe place, as in a padded recovery stall, or a rehab stall with some diversionary equipment or playthings.

I strongly advise that hospitals have some stalls equipped with an adjacent stall, separated by bars, in which a companion animal may be kept such as a pony, or a miniature donkey, or a goat.

Those horses which do not tolerate isolation can be greatly placated by such an arrangement. I have learned that stall vices, such as cribbing and weaving, etc., are not caused as much by confinement as by isolation. I have seen thousands of horses kept in tie stalls. This is common in Europe and in Premarin farms in Canada. It was common when I was a boy when many horses were in tie stalls throughout the winter on Northern farms. Yet, stall vices were relatively uncommon whereas today, in horses kept isolated in box stalls, stall vices are all too common.

Like human hospital patients, and especially children or the elderly, hospitalized horses need to be analyzed, understood, and accommodated on an individual basis.

One special problem needs to be addressed regarding hospital care.

Many horses arrive at a hospital in a horse trailer. Unknown to the staff getting some of those horses into a trailer was a major battle. Unfortunately, many horses are simply not trained to load into a trailer. Worse, many are traumatized when they were trained ineptly, and have become resistant and afraid to load.

Such a horse usually unloads with alacrity, but then, when the hospitalization period has ended, refuses to go back into the trailer and the client usually expects the veterinary personnel to solve the problem.

So, it becomes incumbent upon the hospital to be able to load such a horse. This manual is not the place to teach it, but every hospital needs personnel with the expertise to teach a horse to load willingly and easily. I think the client should be willing to pay for it. Call it "psychotherapy" if necessary.

Where does one learn?

There are a multitude of excellent loading videos out there. One of my favorite is Richard Winters "Foundations." I advise getting it plus one other by any of the many excellent horsemanship clinicians out there such as Pat Parelli, Chris Cox, Dennis Reis, Clinton Anderson and their many contemporaries.

Chapter 10

"Injections"

There was a time when many painful procedures were performed upon both human and animal patients without benefit of anesthesia. Limbs were amputated, abdomens were opened, fractures realigned and skulls trephined in order to relieve pressure. Today, with general and local, and regional anesthesia available, we can scarcely imagine conducting such procedures (let alone experiencing them) without analgesia. Many people today demand general anesthesia for routine dentistry.

Veterinary patients have available to them the same advances in analgesia as do human patients. Since many veterinary patients are potentially dangerous to inflict pain upon, it is to our advantage as well as the patients to use anesthesia to block pain resulting from medical or surgical procedures.

However, one procedure is inevitably painful when performed upon a conscious patient and that is injection. That includes injections given with the express purpose of blocking pain, such as a local and regional anesthesia. Regardless of the purpose, administering any agent via a hypodermic needle into any part of a conscious organism will produce some degree of pain.

So, injection remains as an inevitably painful procedure, to a greater or lesser extent when administered to a conscious and cognizant patient.

How then do we observe the concepts advocated in this publication, of minimizing fear, especially in as reactive and flighty and sensitive an animal as a horse?

The answer is to use techniques which inhibit the detection of pain from injections and there are several ways in which this can be achieved:

1.   Desensitization
2.   Distraction
3.   Speed

Let's consider each of these ways separately:

1.   Desensitization

Happily, there are some horses with a disposition so calm and a pain threshold so high that they show little or no reaction when injected.

In addition, there are <u>many</u> horses that <u>will</u> react somewhat to an injection, but which can be simply and quickly desensitized. When we are talking about injections, we are referring primarily to injections in the cervical area, either subcutaneously, or intramuscularly, or intravenously into the jugular vein. A much smaller number of injections are given into the pectoral, gluteal, or posterior leg muscles, usually because the horse is on a prolonged course of therapy.

Obviously, injections are also given almost everywhere in the body at times for various reasons such as local or regional anesthesia, therapy, etc.

But, percentage wise, a majority of injections will be given in the cervical area.

To desensitize the horse which is somewhat afraid of injection, but not severely so, I was taught to hold the detached needle between thumb and forefinger, pound the area to be injected with the lateral aspect of the fist three or more times, and then rotate the hand and pop the needle

This may work fme for cattle, but it is not a good horse technique. Instead, gently massage and manipulate the site to be injected until the underlying subcutaneous muscle is felt to relax, then, while manipulating and rubbing the skin over the site with one hand, the needle with syringe attached is quietly pushed through the skin. Even for intravenous injections this method will suffice for a majority of horses. As has been repeatedly said, a bit of time, patience, persistence, and an effort to placate the horse pays off.

But, how about the "needle shy" horse for which this method accomplishes nothing? Some of these horses have simply become phobic about injections from past experiences. Others actually have a pain threshold so low that they genuinely <u>feel</u> every injection. I have experimentally blindfolded such horses and using a 26 gage very, very fine needle attempted to stick them to see if their reaction is just phobic, or real. I learned that such horses do indeed feel the needle, however tiny it is. After all, horses feel the bite of a fly!

For most such horses, I learned an injection technique which works most of the time.

For a couple of years ivermectin was available in the USA as an injectable vermifuge. Before it was introduced we learned that it occasionally had a serious and sometimes fatal side effect, and that was Clostridial infection. In fact, that was the reason the injectable drug was finally removed from the market as an equine vermifuge.

However, it was the best drug available at that time, so we decided to use it as part of our parasite control program. But, we were so concerned about the reports of Clostridial infections that we decided to take some extreme precautions. We <u>shaved</u> the injection site. Then, we scrubbed it with a betadine solution for one-hundred strokes. Afterwards, we rinsed it and scrubbed again with an alcohol sponge one-hundred times before injecting. The injection was given with a 1-1/2 inch 18 gage needle.

We did over two and a half thousand injections this way. It actually took as much time as it did to pass a stomach tube, but we experienced two important results:

1.   We never got an infection
2.   With rare exceptions, the horses did not react to the needle

Apparently rubbing the injection site 200 times temporarily desensitized the skin so that the needle was not felt.

Therefore, even after ivermectin injections became obsolete, we effectively handled many needle shy horses by scrubbing the site with an alcohol sponge very rapidly one-hundred or more times.

Still, there are a few horses so hard to inject that the above techniques don't work. For such horses distraction usually solves the problem.

2.   Distraction

Earlier we discussed the lip chain and its varied uses. It can also be used to distract most horses afraid of injections.

To do this, gently and without aggression, place the chain under the horse's upper lip.

Wait for the horse to accept the chain, looking for the relaxation, softening of the eye and lowering of the head. Then, vibrate the chain and give the injection. Usually the horse will focus on the gentle vibration occurring under the lip and will be oblivious to the injection.

If I'm working with an assistant, I will have that person do the vibrating. But, if I'm alone, I do it with one hand and inject with the other. I can even do an intravenous injection this way holding the chain in my left hand, vibrating it, while the thumb occludes the jugular vein. Then, with my other hand I slip the needle into the vein close to my thumb. Most somewhat needle shy horses do not realize they have been needled this way.

In recent years, after I retired from practice, I learned of a distraction technique from one of my former associates, Dr. Richard Stevens.

I own horses and mules and I vaccinate them regularly. The mules, typically, would be suspicious of me for many weeks afterward. I decided that this loss of trust was not worth it and henceforth I would simply "call the vet" to vaccinate my equids, like any layman.

One of my mules, a 16-3 hands tall ex-world champion Western and English show mule was extremely needle shy. Although never aggressive about injections she was physically very powerful and would do whatever necessary to escape a needle.

So, when I asked Dr. Stevens to vaccinate my animals, I told him that I would lock Jordass Jean in a chute. He said,"that won't be necessary. I have a technique for such patients and I never saw you use it."

Skeptically I led "Jeanie" to him. His technician took the lead rope and fed the mule a small hard biscuit. Then, after "Jeanie" finished eating it she was offered a second biscuit, but this time the tech held on tightly to it. A tug-of-war ensued and while the mule attempted to wrest the biscuit from the assistants hands, Dr. Stevens quietly gave her two injections in the cervical area. The mule was completely unaware of the injections.

"They can only think of one thing at a time," he grinned.

I learned something that day. I have used it successfully, by myself since, and am pleased to pass this information on. We often hear the statement "they can only think of one thing at a time". Actually I don't believe this. I think they are simply capable of making a choice. Jeanie may have chosen to ignore a small discomfort in exchange for a large comfort.

3.   The Speed Injection

Those of us who do zoo practice learn to do small injections, like vaccines, so fast that we are gone before the patient can react.

For example, usually using a 2cc disposable plastic syringe with a one inch attached 20 gage needle, we can vaccinate a lion, a tiger, or a leopard, through the cage bars as it walks past us close to the bars. The technique is to hold the syringe between the index and middle fingers and the thumb on top of the syringe plunger. The syringe is then forcefully thrust into the target tissue, the momentum driving the thumb and plunger forward. Enough momentum is used so that the hand bounces back to safety before the startled animal can turn and bite at it. It must be done quickly, with maximum force.

Because the 20 gage needle has sufficient diameter, and because the volume of the injected material is small (usually less than 1-1/2cc), all of it is deposited intramuscularly. With experience and angulation, even subcuticular injections can be given this way. ,

The disadvantage of this method is obvious. Pre-injection aspiration cannot be performed to insure that the needle is not in a blood vessel. However, having given countless thousands of these high speed injections, I have never experienced an inadvertent intravascular injection.

Believe me, you have to do such injections quickly. A wolf, bear, coyote, baboon, or big cat can react with lightening speed.

After doing such injections for years in exotic species in order to immunize them or to immobilize them with immobilizing drugs, we began to use this technique in selected domestic patients.

For example, at public rabies vaccination clinics, some dogs frantically resist being restrained at ground level by their owners. They tumble and whirl and snap. We found that we could quietly sneak up behind such dogs while they were in line and pop them with the vaccine before they were aware what had happened.

It is also a useful technique for the dangerously needle shy horse, the kind that responds to an injection with immediate deadly aggression.

We used to hold vaccination clinics for horse clubs or horse communities during which we would vaccinate many hundreds of horses in a single day.

Typically there was at least one horse in the group so severely needle shy that we could justifiably use the speed injection technique.

Using it in horses requires more than fast eye/hand coordination. The injection should be given as we walk away from the horse.

What we do is stand at the horse's shoulder, the syringe in one hand concealed behind our back.. Stroke the neck with the other hand. Then, turn and walk away, not looking at the horse and simultaneously jabbing him with the syringe. The horse will start and look around angrily, but we are retreating. Predators don't retreat. The horse usually interprets the needle as a fly bite and quickly becomes calm again.

I have repeatedly, in this manual, used the expression "predators don't retreat." I must clarify it. This is the horse's view. A predator retreating is not threatening.

Of course predators retreat! We've all seen dogs and cats run in terror. In Africa I saw a half grown hippopotamus charge a stalking lion. The lion turned and ran in fear. Cape buffalo charge lions and hyenas causing the predators to retreat very quickly.

The horse, a prey creature, can cause us (a predator) to retreat very quickly if we are wise. However, it is an unrecognized novel stimulus, or a recognized stimulus the horse considers predatory, moving TOWARD the horse that will precipitate fight or flight in this species. The same stimulus moving AWAY from the horse allays fear, aborts flight, and gives the horse confidence. That's why I keep saying "predators don't retreat." They don't when their goal is to hurt the horse. If we simply learn to <u>stop</u>, wait, to lean back, to step back, to reassure the horse, to relax, to look down or away, to exhale, to softly stroke the equine patient, to reassure, it will make equine practice so much safer, more pleasant, less confrontational and less stressful.

I will mention one more method of teaching severely needle shy horses to quietly accept an injection, but I want to emphasize how rarely I have used it in practice; probably not more than once a year. However, I demonstrated this method in one of my videos <u>Understanding Horses</u>, (Video Velocity, 1999) on a severely needle shy mare and therefore feel compelled to mention it here. The method involves the Rarey leg strap (or one-leg hobble) and it is time consuming. However, the change in behavior is permanent so perhaps it is worth citing here.

By hobbling one leg, we encourage submissiveness as described earlier. I learned that needle shy horses, if hobbled from anywhere between 5 and 30-minutes, varying with the temperament of the horse, can learn to stand absolutely quiet for the injection. Moreover, they never forget for future injections, as long as they are given in exactly the same place and the same manner.

As described earlier, all we are doing is creating submission via flight control. During my entire career the Rarey leg strap only once failed to cure a needle shy horse. That, of course, was when I was demonstrating it to a group of veterinary students at Mississippi State University. In that case, in order to solve the problem, I had to lay the fully conscious horse down for half an hour and rub her all over the body.

When I let her up this ultimate form of flight control was completely efficacious, allowing me to inject her with no reaction whatsoever. Complete submission had been produced.

John Rarey was the famous 19th century Ohio horse tamer who used the one leg hobble to dramatically change the behavior of formerly intractable horses.

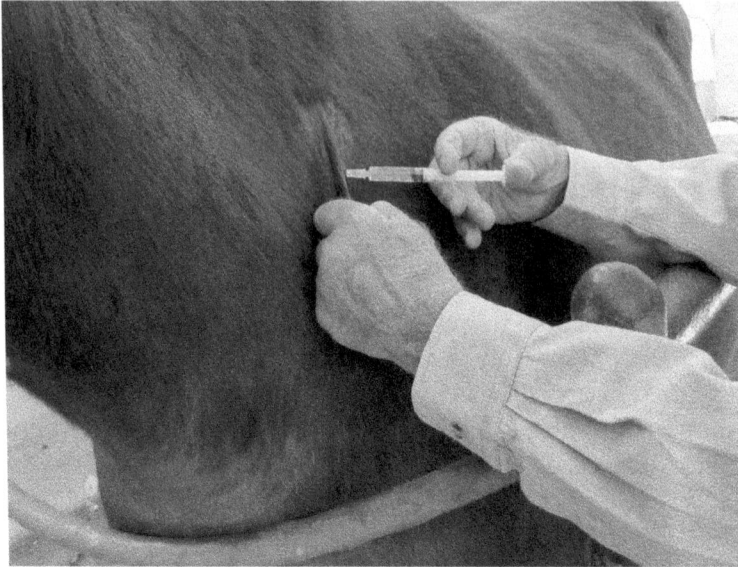

Many horses show not reaction to intra muscular or
subcutaneous injection if the site is massaged a bit, then a
fold of skin is gently manipulated while the injection is
made close to that fold.

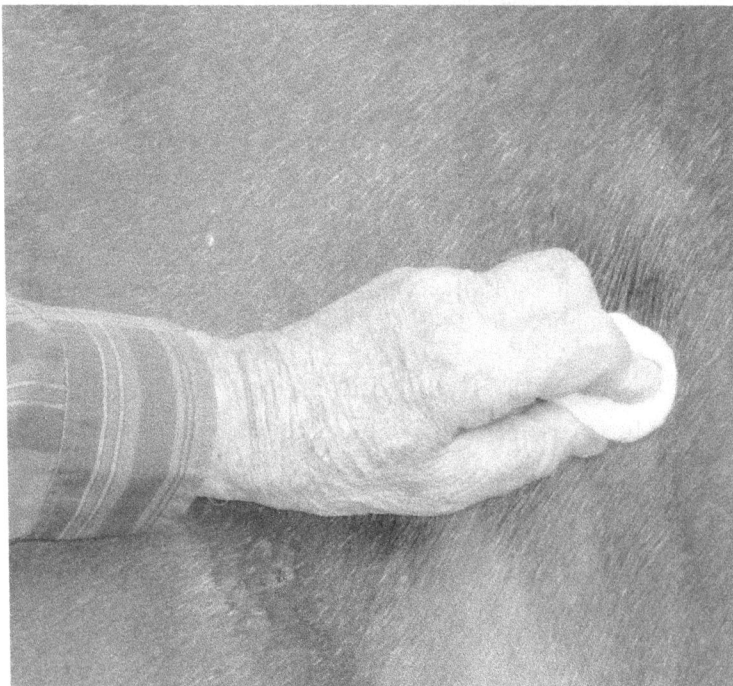

Vigorous rubbing of the injection site, rapidly, for a hundred
strokes will desensitize most marginally needle-shy horses to
an injection. I use alcohol or a betadine solution.

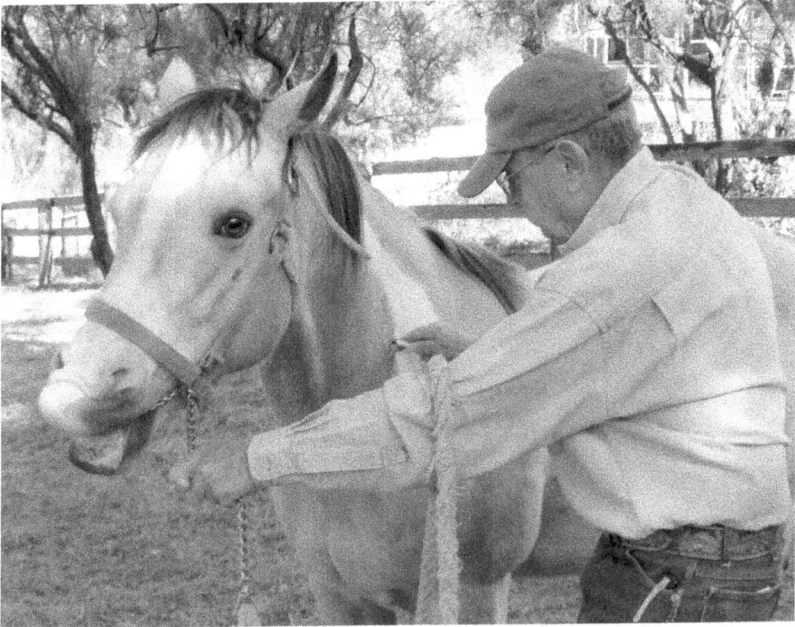

Many needle-shy horses can be restrained using the chain shank under the upper lip with firm pressure applied gently. The effect is similar to that achieved with a Twitch

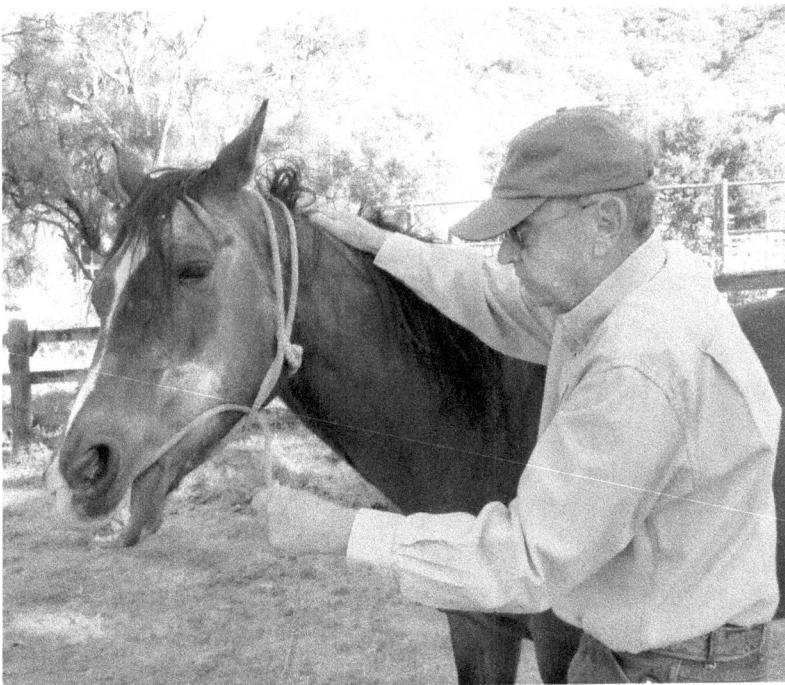

A "War Bridle" above can achieve the same result by putting the loop of rope ordinarily placed over the nose, under the lip

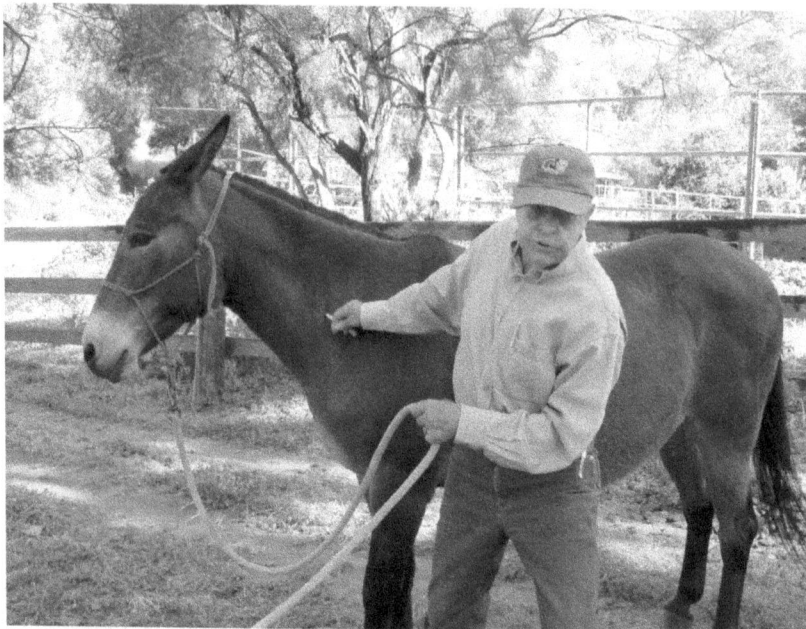

Occasionally the speed injection can be used to fool a needle-shy patient. It takes dexterity and practice to inject as one walks <u>away</u> from the patient. Even though she feels the needle, she does not resist because I am vigorously retreating and not looking at her. Both are non-predatory moves.

Here I am gently vibrating the lip chain to distract the horse. With the same hand I use my thumb to occlude the jugular vein and distend it. Then she is oblivious to the intravenous injection I give with my right hand because her attention is on the vibrating chain.

Chapter 11

"The Assistant"

Since this book is primarily directed at veterinary technicians as well as veterinary students, let's say a few words about the person who may be assisting the doctor while a horse is being treated. Their role is an important one.

I worked alone in my early practice years, or was assisted by the client or somebody who worked at the stable.

Then, as our practice got busier we started having a trained assistant travel with us on our calls. There were no schools of veterinary technology back than, which in England are called "veterinary nursing schools". What we call Licensed Veterinary Technicians are in England, more appropriatately called Registered Veterinary Nurses (RVN).

Eventually we learned that a doctor working alone on a busy day was half as efficient as a doctor working with a properly trained and properly utilized assistant. If, due to the assistant's illness or vacation, one of our doctors had to handle a normal days schedule alone, it would require about twice the number of hours.

However, assistants, whether formally educated or simply trained on the job by the practitioner, must be competent, skilled at handling horses, and diligent.

If things are done correctly, great teamwork can be the result, and this is as it should be.

Sometimes the assistant assists the doctor, and for some procedures the role is reversed.

As mentioned earlier, the assistant should be on the same side of the horse as the person doing the treatment or examination. Of course there are times when this cannot be done, as for example, when the head is being treated or examined.

In any case the assistant should not hold the lead rope too far from the head, with excessive slack in it.

Conversely, a tight grip at the top of the lead rope where it is attached to the halter is also inadequate, and alarms some horses.

To prevent anybody being injured by the horse suddenly swinging its head (and the head of a horse can be a serious weapon), the assistant can hold the cheek piece of the halter. Both the person doctoring the horse and the assistant should be aware of the principal of maintaining body contact with the patient as discussed elsewhere in this manual under "Three Points of Contact".

Chapter 12

"Finale"

By portraying the horse in this publication as the veterinarian's most challenging patient, it is not my intention to discourage veterinarians or veterinary hospital personnel from catering to equine patients.

Historically the horse has been, until relatively recent times, the most important and most traditional of veterinary patients. The horse is a unique creature that has been of immeasurable value historically and culturally, enabling those people blessed with its availability to do things not otherwise possible.

Today, most horses are basically companion animals, and can benefit us emotionally, aesthetically, physically and psychologically.

Equine veterinarians and veterinary personnel usually take great interest in a species they are very fond of and have pride and satisfaction in being able to help that species.

Those who love horses understand what I mean. Those who don't may be perplexed by my emphasis upon the risk that exists in working with such an animal and the precautions I have recommended when handling them.

My goal is certainly not to discourage veterinary students, practitioners, or technicians from working with horses. Actually it is to <u>encourage</u> it, but to do so in a manner which minimizes the stress and/or injury which is so common in veterinary practice to both the humans rendering such service, and to the equine patient itself.

Personally, my preference for horses when the variety of species I have worked with is considered to be clear evidence of my fondness for them. The fact that I handled so many for such a long time is largely the result of the precautions and techniques I have described in this manual. I want to share that knowledge with all those who choose to work with that fascinating and *challenging* animal.

<u>NOTES</u>

<u>NOTES</u>

<u>NOTES</u>

www.ingramcontent.com/pod-product-compliance
Lightning Source LLC
Chambersburg PA
CBHW081200270326
41930CB00014B/3237